Zarrella's Hierarchy of Contagiousness

The Domino Project

Published by Do You Zoom, Inc.

The Domino Project is powered by Amazon. Sign up for updates and free stuff at www.thedominoproject.com.

This is the first edition. If you'd like to suggest a riff for a future edition, please visit our website.

Zarrella, Dan, 1981—

Zarrella's Hierarchy of Contagiousness: The science, design, and engineering of contagious ideas/ Dan Zarrella

p. cm.

ISBN 978-1-936719-24-2

Printed in the United States of America

Zarrella's Hierarchy of Contagiousness

of

Contagiousness

The science, design, and engineering of contagious ideas

By Dan Zarrella

THE
DOMINO
PROJECT
POWERED BY amazon.com

To my wonderful wife and unfair advantage, Alison.

INTRODUCTION

If you've read about social media or been to any marketing conferences, you've probably heard tons of advice like "love your customers," "engage in the conversation," "be yourself," and "make friends." I call this "unicorns-and-rainbows advice." Sure, it sounds good and it probably makes you feel all warm and fuzzy. But it's not actually based on anything more substantial than "truthiness" and guesswork.

Unicorns-and-rainbows advice is the modern-day equivalent of folksy superstitions and old wives' tales. Take a couple of time-honored adages repeated *ad nauseum*, add in the unquestioning awe of an unaware audience, and pretty soon you've got an entire industry based on easy-to-agree-with but unsubstantiated ideas.

But there's a problem. Myths aren't real and superstitions often do more harm than good.

After centuries of superstition in medicine, along came real science—hard facts and real data about what works and what doesn't. Medicine moved out of the Dark Ages, and scientists started making progress in the search for the causes of and cures for diseases. Now it's time for social media to move past mythology and into measurable outcomes.

One of the most important things about the Web is that nearly every interaction can be measured and observed in aggregates of tens and hundreds of millions. We can gather more qualitative and quantitative data about human behavior than ever before. Yet the future of marketing—the very industry that is trying to push communications, business, and public relations forward—is built on advice that is based only on assumptions, clichés, and truisms.

To the snake-oil salespeople, success in using social media isn't something repeatable. It's not the outcome of a process; it's superstition, guessing, and praying.

Those of us who are part of the social media industry now will be the forebearers of the next generation of marketing methods. We're going to be the ones who decide how it plays out. Of course, there aren't any formal degrees in this yet, and most of us don't wear lab coats. But we need to decide if we are going to leave the future of social media to magical tonics, or if we are going to use science and data to discover what really works to motivate people.

To scientists, success in using social media is something you can iterate on, plan for, and learn from. Things that work can be analyzed to produce repeatable, dependable results.

The next time you see or read about or hear someone giving superstitious, feel-good advice about social media, question the person. Ask what data, what science, the advice is based on. Ask the person to prove what he's saying.

And most important, ask yourself: are you a snake-oil salesman or are you a scientist?

Ideas Don't Spread Just Because They're Good

In my previous life at a marketing agency, I sat around lots of conference room tables with bright marketers and businesspeople and was part of a very frustrating line of conversation. It all starts when someone says "let's make something go viral."

The conversation isn't frustrating because I don't like things that "go viral." I love contagious ideas and social media campaigns that work. The conversation is frustrating because of what comes next. When you ask what makes an idea go viral, the first response is that "it's good."

The concept that ideas spread simply because they're good is completely false. There are tons of good ideas that go nowhere, and even more bad ideas that spread like wildfire. There are clearly some other characteristics, some other factors, that determine how much an idea or piece of content will spread.

In his 1976 book *The Selfish Gene*, Richard Dawkins coined the word "meme" to mean a "unit of cultural inheritance." His point was that ideas evolve like genes do, and their success is based on their ability to spread, not on the benefit they provide to their hosts.

Marketers interested in making ideas that spread themselves need to understand those contagiousness factors, and this understanding needs to be based on real science, not on guesswork.

Our World Is Made of Memes

If you've ever seen the *Matrix* movies, you'll remember that their world was composed entirely of computer code. Everything people interacted with was built from computerized instructions. Similarly, our world is made of contagious ideas. Everything made by humans—from the chair you're sitting in, to the book you're reading—exists only because someone had the idea to invent it and that idea caught on, spreading from person to person.

The history of human culture is the history of memes. Politics, religion, wars, literature, and art are all built from building blocks of ideas that succeed in replicating themselves because of their ability to reproduce. Not because they're "good."

Social Media Provide Petri Dishes for Ideas

Biological evolution occurs when there is a population of varied organisms and there is competition for scarce resources. Consider fruit flies; each individual fruit fly is a little different from the rest and they're all competing for a limited amount of food.

Remember the game called "telephone"? One person invents a phrase, whispers it into someone's ear, that person whispers it into the next person's ear, and so on, down a line of kids. The one at the end says what she heard, the originator says what he said, and invariably the phrases are different. Folklorists call the continuous remixing of ideas "communal re-creation." Every person who transmits an idea has an opportunity and often a motive to change the idea to fit his own mental framework. Consider a meme like lolcats. The entire point of the genre is to create new variants, and some—like the "cheezburger" variants—have become more successful than others.

Some of the most contagious brands serve as boxes of crayons, not rubber stamps. Brands that provide their users with a vocabulary and tools that allow them to play with and remix their own ideas succeed because these brands step back and let evolution do what it does best. Examples include campaigns like "South Park Yourself," which lets users customize cartoon characters, and the Doritos "You Make It, We Play It" contest, in which contestants created commercials competing for a Super Bowl spot.

The Variants Best Suited to Selection Pressures Win

In the fruit fly example, the scarce resource is food. Fruit flies with mutations that make them best suited to finding the scarce food are the most successful. For most of human history, the scarce resource constraining the spread of ideas from common person to common person was memory. Until the last few decades, most people did not have the ability to shares ideas with a large number of people. That power was reserved for the rich and powerful. Normal people communicated with their voices, and in order to be able to retell an idea or story orally, you have to be able to remember it.

The oral tradition and Homeric poems reflect this limitation. They're composed of clichéd phrases and mnemonic devices. These poems were created hundreds of years before they were ever written down, so they had to be full of memory tricks to ensure that they could be told for generations, passed on through word of mouth.

Because of the Web and social media, everyone now has the power to type out his ideas and spread them to millions of people. Memory isn't a big problem anymore. You have to be able only to copy and paste a link, not remember an entire epic poem. The change in the environment has introduced a different selection pressure into the mental landscape: attention. There are now so many ideas floating around the Web, they fight for simple awareness.

Reproductive Strategies: Fecundity vs. Longevity

All biological species in existence have developed some form of reproductive strategy. Reproduction strategies have two elements: fecundity and longevity. Fecundity refers to the number of offspring produced in each generation. Fruit flies can have thousands of children in their lifetimes, whereas elephants have only a few. Longevity is the lifespan of an individual. Fruit flies generally live around thirty days, while elephants live for sixty years or more.

If we put these two elements on axes in a quadrant graph, elephants and fruit flies are on opposite sides, but they're both successful. Ideas, too, can be on either side of the chart. If I read and retweet your link, I may think about it for a few minutes, so it won't have a very long lifespan. But it will have high fecundity because I can easily send it to tens of thousands of people on Twitter. On the other side of the graph we find religions. Most religions spread slowly, growing through vertical transmission (parent to child), but once people adopt a religion, they typically follow it for their entire lives.

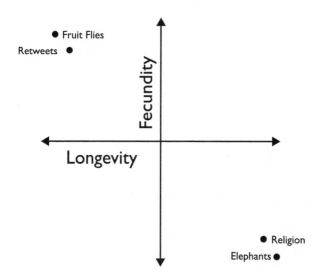

Zarrella's Hierarchy of Contagiousness

Good science involves the search for and development of unifying principles. For social media science, this means developing a framework for understanding the diffusion of ideas and for optimizing our content for contagiousness.

When I began taking martial arts classes a few years ago, my teacher was a big proponent of practical applications and he studied military combat training. He introduced me to the OODA military framework. OODA is an initialism in which the letters stand for the four stages in the combat decision-making process: Observe, Orient, Decide, Act. In every situation, an individual first observes his surroundings and gathers information, then orients this data with his previous experiences. He then decides the best path of action, and finally, he acts.

When I started working alongside a professional sales team, I was exposed to the AIDA concept. It represents the steps in a purchasing decision: Attention, Interest, Desire, and Action. The attention of the customer must be attracted, interest must be raised, desire must be established, and finally, the act of purchasing must be completed.

On the academic side, you're probably familiar with Maslow's Hierarchy of Needs, the pyramid of human needs, depicted with base physical needs on the bottom and self-actualization at the top.

I developed my framework as a model for the decision-making process that happens before someone spreads an idea. This framework describes the three criteria that must be met before someone will spread an idea in any format:

1. The person must be exposed to your content. This means that the person has to be following you on Twitter, be a fan of your page on Facebook, subscribe to your email list, and so on.

2. The person must become aware of your specific piece of content (the idea you want to spread). He has to read your tweet or open your email message.

3. The person must be motivated by something (generally in the content itself) in order to want to share the idea with his contacts.

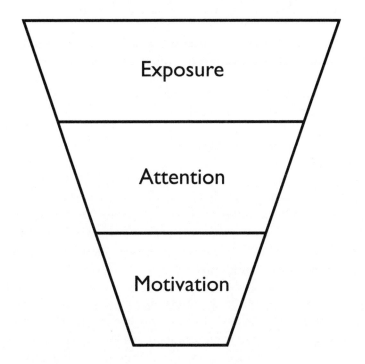

Every piece of content, social network, and campaign has a vastly different conversion rate at each step of this process. For you to understand the scales involved, it helps to visualize a hypothetical set of percentages. If you email nine hundred people, and 20 percent of them notice and open the message, and then 10 percent of those readers forward it to a friend, your email message was shared eighteen times.

At each step, you can change the numbers in your favor:

1. Increase the number of people exposed to your content. Get more email-list subscribers or Twitter followers.

2. Create attention-grabbing content. Do lots of testing on your subject lines to increase open rates.

3. Include powerful calls to action.

The keys to real science are data and experimentation. I've spent nearly five years conducting research into the why, how, and what of contagious ideas. In the next three chapters ("Exposure," "Attention," and "Motivation"), I'll present some of my most important findings and describe how you can use them to optimize your ideas for maximum spread at each step of my hierarchy.

First, I'll explore my key tips for increasing your reach online, including how to get more followers and fans and how to keep them listening to you. Then I'll analyze my data about attention and explain how to develop awareness-grabbing ideas and campaigns to leverage your audience. In the next chapter, I'll present my investigations into what motivates people to spread your ideas.

The last chapter of this book will explain how to begin to conduct your own research and fine-tune the scientifically grounded best practices I've shown you. My goal is to educate you with real data and arm you with effective methodologies so you can take the science of social media to the next level.

EXPOSURE

Before people can spread your idea, they have to be exposed to it. They've got to be following you on Twitter, be fans of your Facebook page, or subscribe to your email list. Seedy peddlers of marketing potions have trunk-loads of advice to sell you—most of it based on what they think sounds reasonable or what they heard their favorite idol say at a conference once. But you and I know better than that. We want real science and hard facts.

Little Seeds Are Lucky Shots

"Viral marketing" isn't a very popular term at the cool New Media kids' table these days. But contemporary "emerging media" folks haven't let any of its delusions go to waste. Consider the notion of the "little seed." The story goes like this: If you've got a contagious idea, and you hand-deliver that idea to a carefully chosen set of people (seeds), each one of them will share it with five or ten friends. And each one of those friends will share it with five or ten more, and so on. Eventually everyone in the world will be a carrier for your cause. Unfortunately, though, this idea is utter nonsense.

The myth tellers who've run the fairy tale ragged tell us about "viral coefficients" and fill our heads with dreams of magnificent stats. It's easy to have a high coefficient if one person shares your video with five thousand of their closest Facebook friends. But that's a single generation, a mere snapshot. Not an empirical average.

Those interested in actual science use a more precise term, borrowed from epidemiology: "reproduction rate." The reproduction rate, or R0 (pronounced "R-naught"), is the number of new infections that a case of a disease will cause in a single generation, averaged over the entire life of the epidemic. If I have a cold and I give that cold to two people, and each of them gives it to two more, the R0 of that cold is two.

It's important to note that this example is calculated based on a population with no immunity to the contagion. Humans can have mental defenses, however. Religion is a great example of memetic immunity. Part of most major religions is a clause stating that other religions are wrong.

With many biological pathogens, R0 is greater than one, meaning that the pathogen spreads to every susceptible person in a population over time. However, every example of idea viruses I've studied, from retweets to email messages, has an R0 well below one. Some pieces of content out there, particularly those that spread through small groups, have a higher R0 for short periods of time. Typically, when those ideas jump into larger populations, the average reproduction rate declines and the ideas die.

The visualization below demonstrates the low R0 of a retweet. Each circle represents a user who tweeted the link from Techcrunch, the size of the circle represents the number of followers they have and the lines indicate they're following someone who tweeted the link before them. You can see that there is an initial burst of seemingly high R0 activity, followed by a longer "die off" period where the reproduction rate falls below 1.

TweetMap of Techcrunch.com's "Startup Life Visualized [Infographic]"

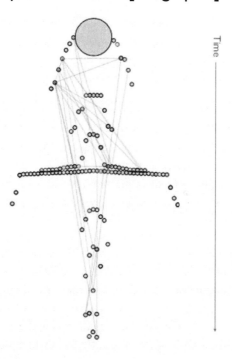

Big Seeds Produce Repeatable Results

A little basic math will show us that seeding our idea to a small number of people and expecting it to take over the world is not realistic. If we have an idea with an R0 of 0.1—which is higher than any idea I've ever studied—and we seed it to ten people, those ten will infect only a single new person, and in the next generation the outbreak will die.

In contrast, if we expose that same idea to 100,000 subjects, the first generation will have 10,000 new people, and the next will have 1,000. In both cases, the idea stops spreading after a while, but with the big seed, the idea reaches far more people before it stops spreading.

Even if you pull off the impossible and come up with an idea with a record-breaking R0 and it spreads like crazy, it's a fluke. I'm not in this game to succeed only when I get lucky, and neither should you be. When combined with science, social media can be a predictable and reliable form of marketing, and great brands aren't built on pipe dreams. Rather than relying on luck, let's focus on doing something repeatable.

The term "big seed" was first coined by researchers Jonah Peretti and Duncan Watts. They conducted an experiment in which they made a banner ad that users could send to their friends by typing email addresses into it. Peretti and Watts then compared two scenarios: one in which they purchased a large media buy and showed the ad to hundreds of thousands of viewers, and one in which they handed the ad to a few select individuals. Unsurprisingly, the big-seed version did far better than the little-seed version. They published the results of their findings in a paper for the Harvard Business Review called "Viral Marketing for the Real World."

Size matters. Don't believe the quacks when they're peddling their snake oil.

Identify Yourself Authoritatively

Have you ever been warned, "don't call yourself a guru"? You'll sound like an arrogant so-and-so, they say. But again, when you look at the data, the rainbow fades.

Effect of Bio Words on Followers

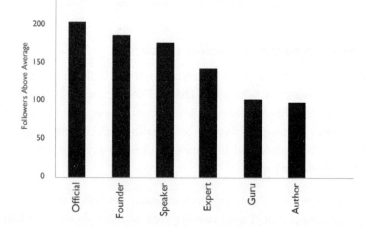

It turns out that Twitter accounts that include the word "guru" in their bios have about a hundred more followers than the average account. The lesson here is not that if you put "guru" in your bio you'll instantly get a hundred more followers—we need to be careful about correlation and causation here—but rather that you should not be afraid to identify yourself authoritatively. Tell people why they should listen to you. In that same study, I found that Twitter users with the confidence to use words like "official," "founder," "author," and "expert" to describe themselves also had more followers than the average. Don't feel limited to using the term "guru."

Think of social media as a networking event. Sure, it can be fun to bounce around and talk to random new people, ignorant of who they are and what they do. But the more I know about your qualifications, the more likely I am to actually listen to you, rather than politely pretend. If you've written a book or founded a company, I want to know.

Negative Remarks Decrease Listeners

Continuing with the cocktail party analogy, we've all had the experience of being stuck talking to a Debbie Downer. I'm sure you know someone like this. Whenever you've got good news, she manages to shut down the usual celebratory conversation with complaints about her life. After a while, you don't want to talk to her anymore, especially not when you're happy.

"Be positive" is a classic unicorns-and-rainbows line, but this time, the data support it. I used two linguistic analysis algorithms (RID and LIWC) to analyze the relationship between negative tweets and follower counts on Twitter. I found that as negativity increased, the number of people interested in reading it decreased. On some level, I wish it weren't true, because there's a certain kind of fun in going out to a bar or restaurant, getting bad service, complaining about it on Twitter, and getting something free. But the data tell me not to make a habit of it.

Effect of Negative Remarks on Follower Count

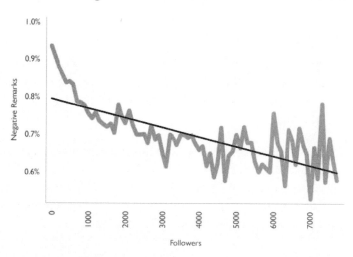

I once presented these data at an open-government conference in Washington, D.C., right around the time of the Gulf oil spill. The audience questioned me on the data. They asked me how I could expect them to be positive about such bad news. My response was to try to find the rays of sunshine, the points of hope in the story. Think of every recent crisis, from the oil spill in the Gulf to the earthquake in Haiti. The most contagious ideas in those cases were the stories of recovery, the calls to text a certain phone number to donate to the relief efforts.

There is no lack of depressing stories on the nightly news. But people don't go on social media sites to get bummed out, especially when they can do that on their couches. We go on social media sites to talk to our friends and generally have a good time. So make me feel good when I hear your ideas; brighten up my little corner of the Web.

Self-Reference Is Not Contagious

Social-media witch doctors fool the masses with exhortations that we only need to be our "authentic selves" online and our adoring fans will flock to us. It works if you're Justin Bieber. But for the rest of us? Let's look at the data.

Using that linguistic system again, this time I analyzed self-referential language on Twitter. I found that the more you talk about yourself, the smaller your audience is. Think about it. You wouldn't stand around and listen to someone pontificate about himself all night long, so why would you expect people to listen to you do it online?

When I've conducted focus groups or surveys about why people read blogs, the respondents have told me the same thing over and over again. What they're interested in is the author's unique point of view, the perspective that only that specific person could have. *Talk as yourself, not about yourself.*

Effect of Self Reference on Follower Count

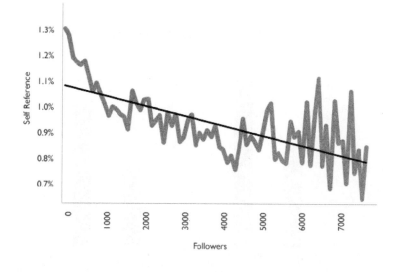

"Engaging in the Conversation" Isn't Everything

The most worn-out myth in all of social media superstition is the old "engage in the conversation" advice. This one really gets under my skin. Everyone with a Facebook friend suddenly thinks he's a social media expert. And this advice is the first magic potion he starts selling. Again, let's look at the data.

When I analyzed the reply rate—the percentage of a user's tweets that start with an "@" sign—I found that users with more than one thousand followers "engage in the conversation" significantly less than those users with smaller audiences. The same holds true for the Twitter celebrities with more than a million followers. People with serious reach on Twitter aren't super conversational.

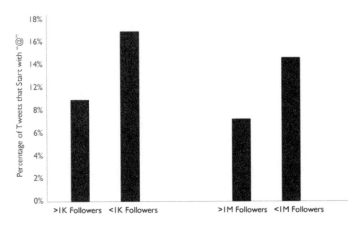

Reply Percentage and Follower Count

I'm not telling you to ignore everyone. Conversation has an important role in customer service and public relations online. I'm warning you not to base your entire strategy on that most precious and pernicious tenet of social media mythology. Nobody cares how chatty you are if you're not adding to the conversation with interesting content.

Influencers Exist

Building reach and getting lots of followers is a great way to start, but that's hard work and I prefer to work smarter. Fans and followers aren't all created equal; some are more influential, more important.

Way back when Twitter was still in its infancy, I conducted a survey asking people how and why they shared content with their friends online. (I didn't have a good word for Twitter users yet; we call them "tweeters" now, but back then I called them "Twits.") Poor word choice aside, folks on Twitter then were bleeding-edge social media dorks. When I asked Twits how often they shared content with their friends in a one-on-one fashion (such as messaging or emailing a link to one person), they reported doing it much more frequently than did non-Twits. And when I asked the Twits how many people they regularly shared content with, they said they talked to many more people than did the less-bleeding-edge respondents.

Content Sharing Frequency

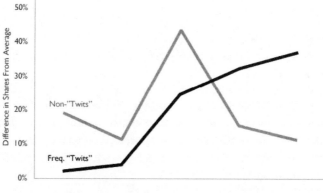

It was those early adopters who shared more content, with more people, more frequently. They were influential. Lots of times I'm talking to marketers in less-than-bleeding-edge industries, like manufacturing, and they complain that their audience isn't hip enough to be on social media sites. And they may be right. Most of their audience isn't checking in on Foursquare or answering questions on Quora. But the segment that is doing those things—however small—is the most influential. Those are the people who'll do the most to spread your ideas. For "mainstream" markets, finding influential users is as easy as being on the newest social media platforms.

Influence Often Comes from Unexpected Places

The traditional way to find influencers online is to look at stuff like reach. And as this chapter has shown, reach is key to spreading ideas. But when we look at actual examples of memes spreading across the social media universe, we find interesting exceptions to the common wisdom. Consider the Nelson Mandela death hoax.

Around 9:40 GMT on a Saturday morning early in 2011, the phrase "RIP Nelson Mandela" began trending worldwide on Twitter. This sparked a wildfire of tweets about his status as dead or alive. This is not the first time death hoaxes have surfaced on Twitter, but it was the first time I noticed one early enough to analyze it to try to find out how it happened.

The first thing I found was that the first person to use the exact phrase that trended was the user named "lebolukewarm." He has since deleted his tweet, but not before it was retweeted at least seventy-one times within just a few minutes. While he wasn't the first to tweet about the rumor, it appears that Tweeter Zero did cause the rumor to "tip" on Twitter. And he had just over a thousand followers when he did it.

One obscure Twitter user isn't the usual picture of influence online. Lebolukewarm couldn't be further from a celebrity. He was in the right place at the right time. And there's very little possibility that even the smartest marketers out there could have predicted that he would have the impact he did.

ATTENTION

Modern, connected people are exposed to thousands or millions of ideas every day. These people don't actually read every tweet or open every email message they get. Before they can spread your idea, it must grab their attention. The second step in my hierarchy of contagiousness is awareness.

The cognitive mechanism of attention involves the prioritization and allocation of the brain's processing resources. The brain decides which ideas are worthy of its precious time. How will your idea fare?

Cut Through the Clutter with New/Old

For many years, thinkers and writers about media and culture have been warning us that we're being deluged with more information than ever before. The mental mess has been piling up for hundreds of years. And advertising executives have been selling their services as a solution to the problem for just as long. They brag to clients that "this campaign" will finally be the one to cut through.

The best clutter-parting tricks to come from big advertising experts are generally of the "buzz" or "guerrilla" marketing variety. Richard Branson challenged Coca-Cola's hegemony by driving a tank up to the soda billboard in Times Square and shooting at it to promote the American launch of his Virgin Cola. This action was intended to cut through the clutter. And sure he got some press and buzz for it, but ultimately the product failed in the US.

Academic researchers working in marketing have been working toward the holy grail of clutter cutting for ages. More recently, a 2002 paper in *Management Science* called "Breaking Through the Clutter: Benefits of Advertisement Originality and Familiarity for Brand Attention and Memory" reported the following:

> *Advertisements that were both original and familiar attracted the largest amount of attention to the advertised brand, which improved subsequent brand memory. In addition, original and familiar ads were found to promote brand memory directly.*

Original and familiar? It sounds contradictory, and on some level, it is. But we can apply the lessons of this research and use the "new/old" strategy. Structure ideas to both arouse attention and stick to memory. Take old content and put it in a new format, or put new content into an old format. Steam punk—in which sci-fi gadgets are constructed from steam-age technology—and the newest *Romeo and Juliet* movie are brilliant examples. My favorite? The book *Tough Love* by John Moore, which is a business book written as a screenplay.

Bigger and Louder Can Work

The most obvious way to get someone to notice what you're saying is to stand on a virtual stool and scream louder than the noise of the crowd. Yelling online means using Caps Lock, loud noises, big fonts, and bright colors. I wish I had data to prove to you that this kind of thing never works. But I don't.

What I do have is data showing that this strategy can work—at least in some instances. A 2006 study by ad-serving network DoubleClick showed that there is a strong correlation between the size of a banner ad and its click-through rate. The bigger an ad, the more it gets clicked on. Sometimes you can be heard more clearly by speaking more loudly.

Personalization Arouses Selective Attention

Have you ever been to a cocktail party so noisy that you can hardly hear the person talking to you from two feet away? But the instant someone across the room says your name, you can hear her clearly. Our senses take in a billion pieces of information every second, but our brain can process only around forty pieces. So we've developed a sophisticated filtering mechanism, called "selective attention," that strains out only the most important bits.

Email marketers have known how to exploit the power of selective attention through personalization for a while. They'll add your name everywhere they can in messages they send you. And even though I know their tricks, this one still works on me.

Name-based personalization is a bit more difficult in social media, but you can speak directly to your audience through the use of words like "you." In 2010, *Fast Company* launched an ambitious but questionably received campaign called "The Influence Project." The point was to measure influence based on how many visitors you could send to their website. When you clicked a button to share the link with your Twitter friends, the tweet that auto-populated included the text "You're more influential than you think." The first time I saw one of those tweets, I thought the sender was talking directly to me. I clicked the link.

Priming Speeds Attentional Processing

Of the billions of bits of information our senses encounter every second, only a portion is recognized. An even lesser percentage actually gets our conscious attention. The faster someone recognizes an idea, the more likely he is to allocate real processing time to it.

Neuropsychology has uncovered a technique for speeding up the processing of certain stimuli in human (and non-human) brains. If a subject is exposed to something related to your idea before he actually encounters your idea, he'll be more sensitive to it, and this makes it easier to catch his attention. The person doesn't even need to be aware of the initial exposure for the priming to work.

The easiest way to make priming work for your idea is to create timely content. If there is a topic or news story currently making the rounds in your target audience, relate your idea to that topic, and the zeitgeist will do the priming for you. Or take a more proactive tack and prepare your Twitter followers, Facebook fans, or email-list subscribers with sneak-peak content about campaigns and ideas you're going to launch soon. Use Hollywood's teaser trailers as a guide.

Avoid the Clutter with Contra-Competitive Timing

Being louder or more attention grabbing through neurological tricks can be hard work. Avoiding the crowd altogether through contra-competitive timing is working smarter.

Every time I publish a new data set, the first section my readers ask about is always timing. I've spent a significant amount of effort on looking at the best times and days to tweet, blog, post to Facebook, and send email. In many cases, the most effective times to send are the less popular times. Because your messages have less clutter to compete with, they break through.

Friday at 4 PM Is the Most Retweetable Time

During my examination of retweets, I first came across the concept of contra-competitive timing. Commercial Twitter activity exhibits a diurnal pattern; that is, it's "awake" during the day and slower at night. Retweet volume shows a later and more exaggerated diurnal wave. It spikes in the late afternoon, around four or five, well after non-retweet activity has peaked for the day. Most tweets happen during the business week, particularly on Wednesday and Thursday, but Friday is when retweet activity is at its highest.

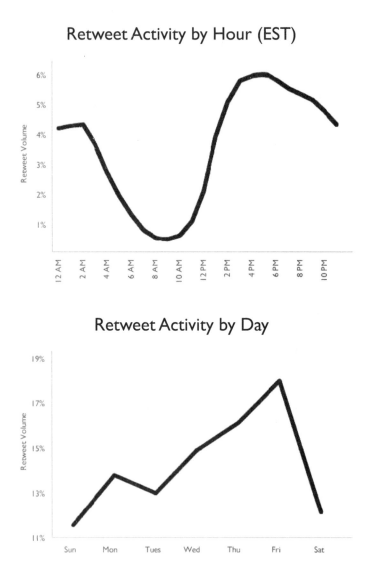

When I look at my TweetDeck columns on Tuesday morning, they're scrolling fast. Each tweet gets much less attention than it does when I look at it Friday evening or even on the weekends. Contra-competitive timing finds moments when Twitter is less competitive and more receptive.

Weekend Stories Get Shared More

Traditional publishing rules instruct writers and editors to avoid publishing important stories on the weekends. This rule leads the majority of mainstream content to be posted during the business week. But Facebook sharing activity gives us a reason to experiment with weekend posting. Although the weekends see less content published on news websites, Facebook sharing is much higher for articles published then. There are also fewer other stories around on the weekends to distract readers.

Facebook Shares by Day

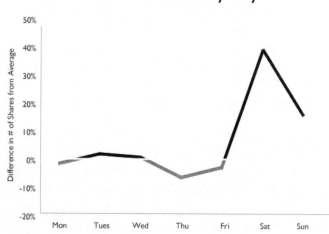

My RSS feed reader delivers new stories faster than I can read them during the week. If I want to get any actual work done, I have to use my scroll wheel to flip through the headlines in the morning, typically spending less than a second on most articles. When I lazily get around to checking out the feed late Saturday morning, I have more breathing room to actually digest the articles and maybe share them on Facebook.

Blog Early for Links, on the Weekends for Comments

One of the questions I'm asked the most is "what are the best times and days to publish blog posts?" In late 2010, I analyzed over 40,000 blogs and looked at three metrics: comments, links, and views.

Comments and views are both highest for stories published around nine or ten in the morning, but posts published two or three hours earlier, at six or seven, tend to get the most links. No special qualifications are required to view a post or leave a comment, but only a certain class of Web users can link to your posts. Rand Fishkin of SEOmoz calls these people the "linkerati." They're most often bloggers. Bloggers tend to get their posts up at nine or ten in the morning, so they can be read by the masses. This means that bloggers are looking for stories to write about and link to before then. If your posts are among the first published in the morning, they'll attract more linking attention.

Posts published earlier in the business week—especially Monday through Thursday—tend to attract the most views and links, but those published on the weekends get the most comments. The principle of contra-competitive timing tells us that there are fewer posts fighting for my attention on Saturday and Sunday, so I have more time to craft a response to your article than I do during the busy week.

Links by Hour (EST)

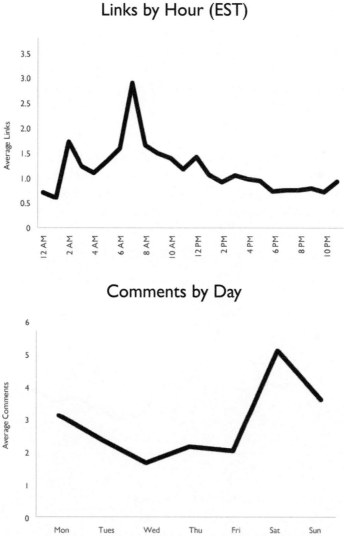

Comments by Day

Send Email Early and on Weekends

Email is the original online social medium, and forwarding is the original retweeting. When I became interested in analyzing email marketing statistics, I emailed my favorite email company, MailChimp, and asked if they had data I could do some investigations with. They came back to me with statistics based on a huge database of nearly 10 billion email sends.

Conventional email marketing commands us to send our messages in the late morning, at ten or eleven. But the massive MailChimp data told me otherwise. Email messages that were sent at five or six in the morning had the highest click-through rates.

CTR by Hour (EST)

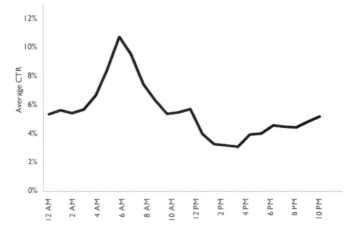

Even more cherished email lore warns against sending email on the weekends, especially when you're dealing with business consumers. Yet again, billions of rows of data made quick work of that myth. Messages sent over weekends had click-through rates twice as high as messages sent during the week. And messages sent on Monday, Tuesday, and Wednesday had the highest unsubscribe rates.

When your email joins the cacophony of newsletters and spam sent during the week, receivers are more likely to get fed up and stop listening to you. But when yours is one of the few commercial email messages they get on Saturday or Sunday, they've got more time to actually read what you're offering.

CTR and Unsubs by Day

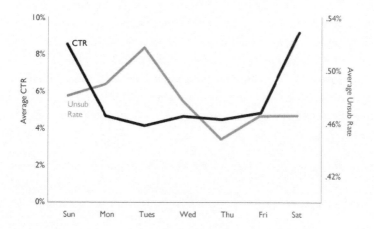

Deliberate Pacing Gets More Attention

As a measure of "attention," I studied Twitter click-through data. The wonderful thing about the bit.ly tool is that its application programming interface (API) allows anyone to view the number of clicks for any bit.ly link, regardless of who made it. I built a database of over 20,000 of the tweets that contained bit.ly links and were issued by twenty of the most followed Twitter users. I then used the API to gather the number of clicks each link had gotten. I calculated an approximate click-through rate (CTR) by dividing the number of times each link was clicked by the number of followers the tweeter had.

I started to notice an interesting trend in the data: the higher the number of links an account tweeted in a given time frame, the lower the CTR on each individual link. And CTR rates varied widely. *The New York Times* account had one of the lowest, while Alyssa Milano had one of the highest. Basically, if an account tweeted one link and then waited at least an hour before sending another one, the CTR was one, but if the account posted two links in the same hour, the CTR was much lower. If the account sent three links, the CTR was even lower. The effect is the same when you use days, rather than hours, as the time unit. Deliberately pacing your content allows each piece to garner more attention.

Data about popular Facebook pages show a similar phenomenon. Pages whose owners posted to their walls once every other day had more fans than did pages whose owners posted more or less frequently.

CTR by Links Tweeted per Hour

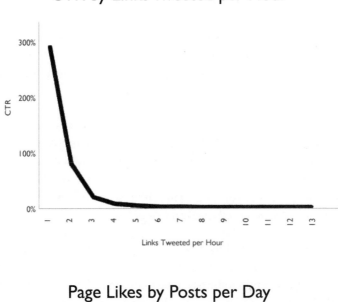

Page Likes by Posts per Day

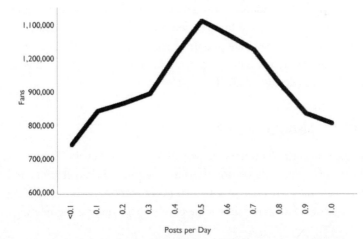

Avoid Information Fatigue

If a hundred links scroll down my screen, I'll give each one of them less attention than if there were only one link. If you post your ideas at the same time a million other marketers do, you're going to arouse far less awareness. This effect is information fatigue, and the solutions are contra-competitive timing and deliberate pacing.

Just as in graphic design, mental white space is key to drawing attention to your ideas. Imagine that you're standing in Times Square looking up at all the glowing, screaming ads. How much attention does even the loudest sign capture? Now picture yourself in the desert, with nothing around for miles but sand and a single billboard. You can simulate this effect through timing and slower posting.

The bottom level of my hierarchy of contagiousness is motivation, and it's the trickiest to achieve. Once someone is exposed to your idea and it catches her attention, she has to be motivated by it to want to share it. This is where you can find the most superstitious advice. People claim that they spread ideas only when those ideas are good, are funny, benefit the world, or conform to some other nebulous standard. So how do we really motivate people to share our ideas? That question is best answered in two parts: Why do people share ideas? And what kinds of ideas do they share the most?

Why Do People Share?

People don't always understand why they do what they do. Thousands of years of evolution have turned us into finely tuned idea catapults, and we're generally unaware of our own inner workings. Understanding why we spread ideas requires some psychosocial reverse engineering.

Reciprocity Trumps Altruism

The unicorns-and-rainbows crowd believes that much human interaction involves altruism. They believe that people do good things for the sake of doing good things. But social science and anthropology have largely discredited that fable.

Proverbs exist as folk knowledge in many cultures. Proverbs are diffused across cultural and language boundaries with surprising ease as cultures adopt sayings from other communities and other languages. In a 1995 book titled *Aging Families and Use of Proverbs for Values Enrichment*, Vera R. Jackson proposed that social exchange theory is an appropriate model for understanding why proverbs are so contagious:

> *Exchange theory suggests that families will continue to do what they found rewarding in the past. If an individual adopts a belief in a proverb, and receives a certain amount of pleasure (healthy or unhealthy), that individual will be more inclined to share the proverb with other family members. Moreover, once there is family acceptance of a proverb, families are less likely to consider other proverbs outside of those they already believe in.*

Instead, the academic literature gives us a theory of social exchange wherein every interaction between two people is an exchange of value. In the case of ideas, what is valued is information. The seminal work on the topic is by a gentleman named George Homans. In his paper "Social Behavior as Exchange" (*American Journal of Sociology*, Vol. 63, No. 6, May 1958, pp. 597–606), he tells us that "... the more valuable the sentiment or activity the members exchange with one another, the greater the average frequency of interaction of the members." Furthermore, "... the greater the reinforcement, the more often is the reinforced behavior emitted. The more cohesive a group, too, the greater the change that members can produce in the behavior of other members in the direction of rendering these activities more valuable."

In social media, your audience has the same motivation it's had for thousands of years. They want to share information with the friends and family that will give them the reputation of being a valuable person to interact with. So give it to them.

Reputation-Enhancing Content Gets Spread

When I asked people why they share ideas with their friends, they consistently told me that they wanted to build a reputation as a thought leader. This would ensure that people would share valuable scarce information reciprocally with them. It's not about altruism, then; it's about reciprocity.

Unlike what the unicorns-and-rainbows people will tell you, everyone isn't just "being themselves" in social media. The average Facebook user has 130 friends. That's an audience. If you've ever done any public speaking, you know that being in front of even a handful of people turns on your self-awareness. Every social Web denizen knows that everything you do online will be seen by someone, even those who you wish wouldn't pay attention. If your ideas reinforce my reputation, I'll share them.

Banal Information Is Not Transmissible

Scientia potentia est. Knowledge is power. We've all heard it, but it's not really that simple. Information that everyone has isn't powerful.

Information that is scarce is powerful. Imagine you're a caveman. If you know the best hunting ground or berry-picking field, that's valuable. But if every tribe in a 50-mile radius also knows about it, it loses its power. The saying should really be: scarce knowledge is power.

In my surveys, respondents have explicitly told me that they pass information on to friends who would otherwise not get it. They never told me they'd share the same information everyone had heard thirty times before. They did tell me they preferred to share news-based content, rather than humor or opinion. Breaking news is scarce. And when I looked at retweets, I found that they contained fewer common words than original tweets did.

Word Novelty in Retweets

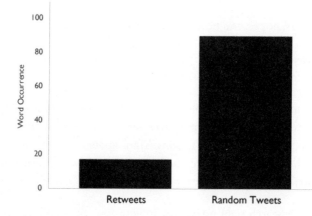

Rumors Spread in Information Voids

During World War II, the British intelligence agency MI6 and their American counterparts in the OSS (which eventually became the CIA) created programs designed to weaponize rumors against the Nazis. MI6 and the OSS enlisted the help of an academic named Robert Knapp to help them study and understand how they could make their propaganda contagious. Over the past few decades, their research has become declassified. And it's a gold mine for marketers interested in engineering memes. The declassified reports detailed certain kinds of information that one should gather before designing a rumor for a specific group. This information included:

1. The kinds of information the group is eager for

2. What information the group already has and what it lacks

3. The fears, hopes, and hostilities the group already has

4. Customary and traditional ways in which the group deals with those fears, hopes, and hostilities

If the locals in a village heard a big boom one day, a rumor could easily be constructed to explain it if the authorities did not. Sociologists explain rumors as collective sense-making. Think about the Tiger Woods scandal or the iPad. In each case, there was a gap in the authoritative explanation for some period of time, and rumors filled in that gap.

Go to Twitter Search right now. Type in your keywords followed by a question mark. You'll find hundreds or thousands of information voids. Each one of these questions tells you exactly what kind of information people are hungry for. Fill knowledge gaps with your ideas.

Information Can Ensure that Safety Is Shared

Remember your Paleolithic self. This time, let's say you know that a certain kind of berry is poisonous. If you fail to share this information with your tribe, many of them may die. You'll then have a much harder time surviving and reproducing. Thus, sharing knowledge like this is a self-defense mechanism.

Urban legends contain covert warnings. One of my favorites is the story of the serial killer on Lover's Lane. A boyfriend and girlfriend are out late one night, necking in the boy's parents' car on a scenic but deserted back road. On the radio comes an emergency broadcast warning about a one-handed lunatic escapee from a local asylum. The girl gets scared and doesn't want to get frisky anymore. Frustrated, the boy starts the car and peels out, taking her home. When she gets out of his car, she notices a bloody hook hanging from the passenger-side door handle.

Did you get chills reading that last line? The effect is called "delayed orientation." The story leaves out one key piece of information, which is revealed to the protagonists (and the listener) too late to do any good. Your Paleo mind is engineered to react to information like this because you need to know which berries will be fatal before it's too late. This legend's underlying warning is to never make out with your sweetheart—because a psycho killer may get you, and your parents will be unhappy.

People often circulate email messages with warnings about the latest virus or worm making the rounds. Unbeknownst to the senders, however, the warnings are often hoaxes (trying, say, to get you to delete a system file that is actually benign), and the viruses are nonexistent or not terribly destructive. Of course we all want to be careful with our computer systems. But for our purposes, the useful point is that for every virus or worm spreading through the Internet, I get warned against it probably a hundred times. *The warnings are far more contagious than the actual viruses.*

Just like virus warnings, any information that can protect readers from harm, like a great deals website preventing people from paying too much for a product, will get shared as a form of self-defense.

The Human Mind Is an Imitation Engine

"Monkey see, monkey do" might be fun to imagine, but the reality of the matter is that humans are much better at imitation. In fact, playing copycat is mostly how we learn languages, behaviors, and skills. You're in a boring class or a serious meeting. Someone quietly yawns. Then another person does, and another. Soon enough you're struggling to keep your mouth closed and your eyes open. Even when we're not doing it on purpose, humans are designed to imitate each other.

In 1962, a few weeks after Tanzania gained its independence, three teenage girls in a boarding school in an isolated village began laughing. According to a 1963 report, a total of 10,000 adult men and women and teens of both sexes caught the "disease" after coming in contact with an infected person. The epidemic is regarded as case of mass psychogenic illness. The modern explanations revolve around the intense religious and cultural changes that were happening to the town due to its newfound independence and the replacement of old spiritual beliefs with Western religion. The laughter acted as a collective catharsis.

The whole country was tense, and when people saw someone else let go and start laughing, it flipped a switch, and suddenly they could laugh, too.

Neurologists have even begun to investigate actual imitation "hardware." A kind of brain cell called a "mirror neuron" activates the same way when a person sees someone else take an action as when this person takes the action himself.

Social Proof Makes Ideas Safe to Transmit

In his 1998 book *Influence*, Robert Cialdini popularized the concept of social proof, or imitation on the cultural level. He said that we believe an action to be correct as we see other people perform that action. Imagine two restaurants on a street in a city you've never been to. One has a huge line outside and the other is empty. Which restaurant do you think has the best food?

Economists call this phenomenon an information cascade. The first person to come across those two restaurants made a random choice and lined up in front of one restaurant. Another person came along, and that one-person line gave a signal to choose that place. The third person saw two people lined up and the signal was twice as strong. Each new person joining the line made it seem more obvious where the best food was. We assume that people who make choices before we do have more information than we do, so we imitate. The same thing happens on the web when a new website starts building readership and gets mentioned by all our favorite internet celebrities.

The science behind this idea has been presented in rigorous detail in a variety of academic papers. One paper, titled "Theory of Fads, Fashion, Custom, and Cultural Change as Informational Cascades," by Sushil Bikhchandani, David Hirshleifer, and Ivo Welch (*The Journal of Political Economy*, Vol. 100, No. 5, Oct. 1992, pp. 992–1026), defines information cascades:

> *An informational cascade occurs when it is optimal for an individual, having observed the actions of those ahead of him, to follow the behavior of the preceding individual without regard to his own information.*

A 1980 paper by John Conlisk titled "Costly Optimizers versus Cheap Imitators" (*Journal of Economic Behavior & Organization*, 1980, Vol. 1, Issue 3, pp. 275–293) showed that "imitators may have as high a long-run 'fitness' as optimizers." In 1992, Peter J. Richerson and Robert Boyd published a paper called "Cultural Inheritance and Evolutionary Ecology" (*Ecology, Evolution, and Human Behavior*, Aldine de Gruyter, NY, pp. 62–92), which showed that in many instances, social learning (like imitating your peers) is rewarded by natural selection. Optimizers go out to the forest and eat every new fruit they see, finding out which fruits are safe through a dangerous game of trial and error. Imitators follow optimizers around and learn from their mistakes.

Social Proof vs. Novelty

For years, I gave talks in which I proclaimed the importance of leveraging social proof in online marketing. I told people to show off, at every opportunity, the number of comments, tweets, and Facebook shares their blog posts got. At some point I realized I was violating my own cardinal rule and was just giving advice based on what sounded right, not on sober examination.

So I did a couple of experiments. I Photoshopped two fake Tweet buttons. One button said that a post hadn't been tweeted yet, and the other button said that the post had been tweeted 776 times. Then I split-tested them against each other. I showed half the people who viewed an article one button, and half the other. I expected that the 776-tweets button would get clicked way more.

I was wrong. The zero-tweets button was clicked more than double the number of times the 776-tweets button was. Shocked, I repeated the experiment with faked RSS subscription numbers. With a lower degree of statistical significance, visitors seemed to prefer the image that said that my site had tons of subscribers.

Experiment #1:	0 tweets	vs.	776 tweets
	tweet		retweet
Impressions:	4141		4177
Clicks:	18		8
CTR:	.43%		.19%

97.63% Confidence

It turns out that social proof and novelty are nuanced phenomena that work together. In some circles, people know my site and my content; I already have some level of social proof. Those people know that if they share my posts, there isn't much risk that they'll be sharing bad stuff. I've been pre-selected. But they want to be the first person to share a new post, not the 778th.

Audiences Evangelize Underdogs

In folklore there is a standard plot: huge powerful entity abuses little guy; little guy fights back and wins, and the audience cheers. This rooting for the little guy is called the Goliath Effect. Stories from *Braveheart* to *The Mighty Ducks* are based on this pattern.

If we boil down the story's most fundamental structure, we can say that the "villain" is "wronging" the "victim." Let's say "big corporations are polluting the ocean." You're less powerful than a big corporation, and if you believe the ocean is something that needs to be saved, you can't do it by yourself. You need to spread the idea and recruit others to help you take on Goliath. It's a devilishly simple contagious idea. Apple did this brilliantly from the start. Steve Jobs warned against the abuses of IBM in the early days, and of Microsoft, more recently.

One of the most popular posts on my blog over the past four years bore the title "Twitter Plans to Mangle Retweets." The way retweets functioned was about to be changed, and in my eyes the change was for the worse. Tweets were the victim and Twitter was the villain. I called my readers to action to gang up to try to save Twitter. That post went viral.

Aim for Combined Relevance

I'm interested in marketing and science. I also love watching zombie movies. All of my friends know this, and I've mentioned it to countless audiences over the years. Every time someone writes an article about marketing lessons learned from zombies, it finds its way to my inbox a few hundred times. I once returned to my office after a speaking engagement to find a thank-you gift waiting for me. Inside the box was a zombie scientist action figure.

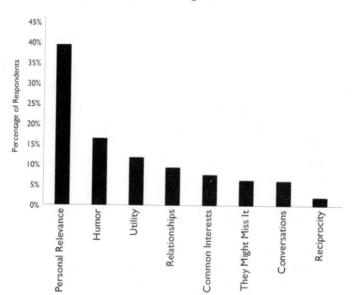

Content Sharing Motivations

Every time I conduct a survey or focus group and ask people why they spread ideas, the number-one answer is always "relevance." People say things like "an article reminds me of a friend" or "it seems right up so-and-so's alley." I could take the lazy way out and tell you to "be more relevant," but that's too nebulous to be useful. Instead, let's try something I call "combined relevance."

A few years ago, I was experimenting with a social news website called Digg. I was in the shower one morning and had an idea. What if someone invented a USB absinthe spoon? In case you've never heard of it, absinthe is a strong, turn-of-the-century alcohol enjoyed by the likes of Vincent Van Gogh and Oscar Wilde. To make it more palatable, a ritual exists to mix sugar into it, using fancy slotted spoons.

I got out of the shower, registered a domain, found an image of an absinthe spoon, and Photoshopped a USB connector onto the spoon's handle. I wrote a cryptic message on the site, something along the lines of "They said we couldn't do it, but we did. Now we need to know why you're cool enough to get one of the first prototypes." Within twenty-four hours there were more than five hundred comments pleading for a prototype. It was featured on the top gadget blogs, Gizmodo and Engadget. By that evening, I was fielding calls from small-town TV stations filming weirdest-gadget segments.

It turns out that there are a lot of geeks who are into gadgets and absinthe. By blending these two seemingly discrete interests, I had created what I call "combined relevance." When someone who was into both of those things, or knew someone who was, saw my absinthe spoon gadget, he knew it was right up his alley and he had to have one. And he had to tell all of his likeminded friends about it.

What Do People Share?

Now that we've got an understanding of the real reasons people spread ideas, let's talk about what kinds of ideas they share the most.

Uncomplicated Language Is Contagious

Readability tests are designed to measure the reading grade level required to understand a specific piece of content. The higher the score, the more complex the language is. The most popular readability test is called the Flesch-Kincaid test and is built into Microsoft Word.

While studying Facebook sharing, I gathered a database of stories published in a variety of popular news sources, including geeky places, like Mashable and TechCrunch, and mainstream outlets, such as CNN and *The New York Times*. I measured how readable each story was and how many times it was shared on Facebook. I found an inverse correlation between the complexity of the articles and the number of times they were shared. As stories became more challenging to read, they were posted to Facebook less often.

I also explored the parts of speech in the titles of those same articles. I determined that the use of flowery, adverb – and adjective-laden language was related to lower sharing rates. As Strunk and White told us decades ago in their book, *Elements of Style*:

> *Write with nouns and verbs, not with adjectives and adverbs. The adjective hasn't been built that can pull a weak or inaccurate noun out of a tight place... it is nouns and verbs, not their assistants, that give good writing its toughness and color.*

Sharing by Readability

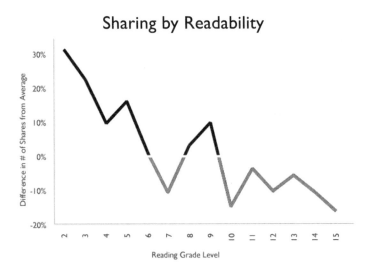

Shares by Part of Speech

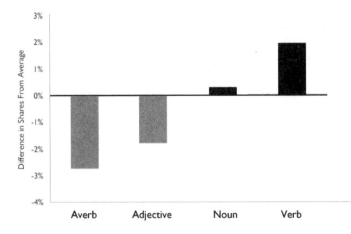

The Most and Least Retweetable Words

Perhaps my favorite data set is my giant MySQL table of 100 million retweets. A while ago, I pulled out of that table a list of the most "retweetable" words and phrases. I found twenty words that occurred more often in retweets than they did in non-contagious tweets. I also pulled out the least retweetable words, or what I call "viral kryptonite." I've presented these lists at events probably a hundred times, and at nearly every event, someone will come up to me afterwards with his phone out and show me how cleverly he smooshed all the words together to make the world's most (or least) retweetable tweet. It is invariably meaningless. The funny part is that when I tell the person to check his mentions, he often finds that he has actually gotten retweeted.

The list of the most retweetable words is topped by the word "you." People don't want to hear about you; they want to hear you talk about them. Tweets that tell people how they can do things and learn things do very well. The list also contains phrases like "how to" and "top 10." These phrases indicate that the content they point to is broken up into manageable chunks rather than being huge blocks of intimidating text.

The best phrase on the list, however, is "please retweet." You should see the unicorn folks freak out about this one. They tell me that it sounds too desperate, demanding, and downright wrong. But it works. Try it out right now. Irving Kirsch, a researcher at the University of Connecticut backed me up in a recent experiment. He gave some subjects hypnotic instructions to mail thirty postcards, once a day. And just nicely asked another group to do so. "Please mail these." The second group complied with the request more often. Social requests are just as powerful as full-on hypnotic trances.

On the flip side of the coin are the least retweetable words. Drivel like "tired," "bored," "watching," and "game." Words that indicate people narrating particularly boring parts of their lives. Of course I'm not going to retweet those.

Most Retweetable

1. you
2. twitter
3. please
4. retweet
5. post
6. blog
7. social
8. free
9. media
10. help
11. please retweet
12. great
13. social media
14. 10
15. follow
16. how to
17. top
18. blog post
19. check out
20. new blog post

Least Retweetable

1. game
2. going
3. haha
4. lol
5. but
6. watching
7. work
8. home
9. night
10. bed
11. well
12. sleep
13. gonna
14. hey
15. tomorrow
16. tired
17. some
18. back
19. bored
20. listening

The Most and Least Shareable Words

To come up with similar lists for Facebook, I looked at words in articles shared on Facebook and found the words that correlated most strongly with those articles being shared more often or less often. There are some significant differences between these lists and the Twitter word lists because the Facebook audience is a much more mainstream one.

The list of most shareable words is headed by the word "Facebook." Yep, Facebookers love talking about Facebook. The rest of the list was mostly stuff you'd hear on the nightly news. Political words and phrases like "Obama" and "health care." Most interesting, the words "why" and "how" do very well. Online, people want to get deeper into stories than they can with the thirty-second sound bite they heard on TV.

The list of least shareable words is full of social media dork words. Stuff like "apps," "social," and "Twitter." Everyone is on Facebook. Both your mom and your college roommate are, and most Facebook users aren't into every bleeding-edge New Media website like you are.

Most Shareable

1. facebook
2. why
3. most
4. how
5. health
6. bill
7. big
8. best
9. video
10. you
11. apple
12. media
13. top
14. obama

Least Shareable

1. vs
2. apps
3. review
4. down
5. poll
6. game
7. york
8. twitter
9. social
10. time
11. iphone
12. google
13. tv
14. live

CONCLUSION

So now that you see what kinds of data are available, where do you go from here? Use the information presented here as a starting point, and then do your own tests and generate your own data.

The Scientific Method Demystifies Contagious Idea Creation

Nobody can predict the future on gut feelings alone. You can't effectively guess whether or not a piece of content is going to go viral. But you can test. Experimentation is the only way to produce reliably contagious ideas, and the scientific method should guide your experiments.

For our purposes, we can break the scientific method into four steps:

1. Define your goals.

2. Research your audience.

3. Prototype content ideas.

4. Test your content.

Define Your Goals

If you're planning to use social media in your marketing, hopefully you have an understanding of what you want to get out of it. If you don't? It's time to set some goals. If you don't know where you're trying to go, there's no way you can figure out how to get there. In most cases, your goals should be generating real business and actual money. But in some cases, you'll be looking for some other return on your investment in social media.

Whatever your goals are (sales, leads, brand awareness, or buzz), set specific, quantifiable targets. Use actual numbers. Say you want to generate $10,000 in new sales this month, or 1000 new leads. Goals are worthless if you can't fail to achieve them.

Research Your Audience

Researching your audience includes understanding the demographics, preferences, and behaviors of the entire group you'd like to reach, as well as identifying the most influential and connected parts of your audience. Generally, the influencers are early adopters and savvy social media users.

The easiest way to research your audience is with a survey or focus group. Ask current customers what sites they read, what kinds of content they like, what information they're missing, and how they choose to read a specific blog, follow a specific Twitter account, or like a specific page. If you're using a survey, allow people to answer with free-form text entry fields, and then read each comment. You'll find common themes. Conduct your own qualitative investigations to move from general, scientifically grounded best practices to industry-specific knowledge.

Use Best Practices as Starting Points

There are two kinds of scientific research, best exemplified by medicine and physics. In physics, there are laws. Gravity always works the same way. Medical research, on the other hand, is based on data sets of thousands or millions of subjects. Courses of treatment are recommended by the research. For individual patients, doctors start with the best practices and customize them to specific cases and needs.

Social media science is more like medical research than like physics. And as with medicine, these best practices are starting points that work in the majority of cases, but they should be viewed only as starting points. The points uncovered with data are potential solutions to be tested in your specific case. The best data are always data you've gathered yourself.

Use the best-practices data to create prototypes of your ideas. Follow the rules I've laid out in this book to make a short video, blog post, tweet, or status update. Don't get hung up on long-form content, and don't polish yet. Instead, focus on building as many variations of your ideas as possible.

Experiment Evolutionarily

Evolution is how contagious ideas are created in the wild. Where there are lots of different ideas, and there is competition for mind space, only the most effective ideas will win. Social media platforms are the most powerful memetic petri dishes in history, nurturing the growth and spread of virulent ideas, because of the plethora of ideas, the size of the audience, and the speed of spreading.

Take advantage. Conduct your own evolution. Release your prototypes into the wild as fast as you can. Measure the right things, and you'll quickly learn what works and what doesn't. Then take those elements that succeeded and iterate on them with your larger and longer campaigns.

Measure Your ROI

The most odious social media myth I've ever heard is that you cannot measure the return on investment (ROI) of social media. "What is the ROI of putting your pants on?" is my favorite version. To argue that the future of marketing is beyond—or above—effective measurement and monetary justification is insulting. You can, and should, measure how much money your investments in social media are making for your business.

In fact, if you're not measuring it, you're doing something very, very wrong.

Keep in mind, however, that Web analytics is about precision., not accuracy Accuracy is about measuring every single possible action, precision is about establishing a baseline of activity and monitoring changes from there. There will be some activity you can't track. It's just the nature of the Web. But the numbers that fall through the cracks are the exception, not the rule. Getting simple referral reports from a free analytics provider (such as Google Analytics) is a great first step in measuring how many sales, leads, or impressions (if you're selling ad space) social media traffic is driving. Using tracking tokens on these sites can make those measurements even more precise.

If you're selling products online and have a direct path to conversion, as with an e-commerce site with a checkout process, it should be easy to measure the real fiscal results of your efforts. If you're trying to generate leads, have closed-loop analytics systems in place to track which visitors ended up becoming customers.

Use Leading Indicator Metrics

Once you're actually measuring how much money social media activity is making you, you can start to look at other metrics. They're leading indicators that your campaigns are about to produce actual monetary value.

The first place to start with these early metrics is with referral traffic to your site from social media platforms. How many visitors is Twitter sending? And use the engagement metrics on those visits: How many pages does the average Facebook visitor view on your site? Think about clicks on links you're posting to external sites as a measurement of how much attention each link is getting.

You can also measure your success based on reach. How many followers and fans do you have? How many people are subscribed to your email lists?

Also think about measuring specific ideas on their contagiousness. How many likes did your last Facebook post get? How many times was your last Twitter update retweeted?

Question Experts

Now you know better. You know how to see through the unicorns-and-rainbows myths. Don't listen to the snake-oil salesmen when they deceive you with their prescriptions for exotic tonics. You have science now.

Marketing shouldn't be based on luck. You can produce results from social media that are reliable and repeatable. You have control. And you're way ahead of the curve. Most marketers (and probably your competitors) aren't thinking this way yet.

When I first started down the path of science and I began to see beyond the myths, I was angry. I felt lied to by the marketing idols I had looked up to. But then I realized that they're not spewing bad advice to be malicious. They're doing it because it's all they know. Don't get angry. Just realize that it's your duty to help people move into the modern world of scientific marketing.

The next time you hear a social media myth, question it. Ask for the proof, and ask out loud.

THANKS

to the companies that helped sponsor this book

Acknowledgments

Lots of people helped with this book and the work I've done on it over the years, and I'm sure to forget someone, but here goes.

Thank you,

To all the HubSpot folks, especially Kipp Bodnar, Mike Volpe, Jeanne Hopkins, Brian Halligan, Dharmesh Shah, Brian Whalley, Magdalena Georgieva, Tom Cattaneo and Eric Vreeland.

To the great folks at The Domino Project, especially Seth Godin, and Willie Jackson.

To my industry friends Shira Lazar, Brian Simpson, Mari Smith, Guy Kawasaki, Brett Tabke, and Nancy Duarte.

About The Domino Project

Books worth buying are books worth sharing. We hope you'll find someone to give this copy to. You can find more about what we're up to at www.thedominoproject.com.

Here are three ways you can spread the ideas in this manifesto:

1. Hold a discussion group in your office. Get people to read the book and come in and argue about it. How open is your company to innovation and failure? What will you do if your competitors get better at it than you are?

2. Give away copies. Lots of them. It turns out that when everyone in a group reads the same thing, conversations go differently.

3. Write the names of some of your peers on the inside back cover of this book (or scrawl them on a Post-it on your Kindle). As each person reads the book, have them scratch off their name and add someone else's.

Tweet your thoughts: #dominoZ

We hope you'll share.

About the Cover

Bunnies! Not unicorns or rainbows, but of course, bunnies.

Great ideas spread and multiply.

You get the idea. Be fruitful.